T0345307

THE VIRTUES OF DISILLUSIONMENT

$$(-1)$$

$$\times$$

$$(-1)$$

$$=$$

$$+1$$

The Virtues of Disillusionment

Steven Heighton

◊ AU PRESS

FOREWORD

IN JANUARY 2020, Steven Heighton launched the tenth anniversary year of Athabasca University's writer-in-residence program with a public presentation of this profound meditation on the nature of illusion and disillusionment. Over the previous decade, the program has hosted a wealth of accomplished Canadian writers: Joseph Boyden, Tololwa M. Mollel, Hiromi Goto, Tim Bowling, Anita Rau Badami, Esi Edugyan, John Vaillant, Richard Van Camp, and Katherena Vermette. In this role, the authors spend sixty percent of their time working on their own writing projects and forty percent as a resource for Athabasca University's students, staff, faculty, and alumni.

Each resident author has provided generous and enthusiastic feedback on the work-in-progress of our community's creative writers, thereby inspiring and guiding the completion (and sometimes publication) of poems, short stories, essays, and novels. Our AU authors have also made impressive use of the personal creative time generated by this position. In the years immediately following an AU residency, writers have published award-winning books such as Joseph Boyden's *The Orenda*, Tim Bowling's *The Heavy Bear*, Esi Edugyen's *Washington Black*, and Richard Van Camp's *Moccasin Square Gardens*.

In addition to mentorship and writing time, the AU writer-in-residence program offers the opportunity for chosen writers to engage with AU's community in two public talks about specific issues surrounding a current work-in-progress or about more general insights concerning the literary craft. Over the years, live and virtual audiences have been treated to a wide range of approaches to this component of the residency. The authors' talks have ranged from sneak peaks at works-in-progress, to intimate accounts of the motivation behind a literary project, to intellectual explorations of creativity and the role of art, to inspiring tips on the writing process. The luxury of two talks during one residency means that even the same author can put a very different slant on this direct engagement with the AU audience.

In John Vaillant's first talk, presented shortly after the election of Donald Trump as President of the United States of America, Vaillant offered an intimate and emotional discussion of how artists can continue to find their muse in the midst of relentlessly negative and alarming news cycles. In his second AU event, Vaillant spoke less as an artist and more as a journalist, less about inspiration and more about process, sharing details of the extensive and rigorous research he conducted in Fort McMurray for his forthcoming book *Fire Weather*. Other writers have kept our audiences riveted with explorations of the points to consider when writing dialect and slang, the inspiration provided by family history and photographs, and the different challenges and rewards of writing poetry versus writing fiction.

When our staff, faculty, and students filled the conference room at AU's Peace Hills Tower in downtown Edmonton to hear Steven Heighton's 2020 writer-in-residence talk about illusion and disillusionment, we did so with a sense of anticipation created by the quality of previous talks and the accomplishments of our current writer. Steven Heighton exceeded expectations with his deep dive into the role of ego in the writer's life, the misguided nature of writing in pursuit of attention, and the distinction between hope-free and hopeless as it applies to athletic performance and literary ambition (and, actually, to all ambition).

STEVEN HEIGHTON is the author of over fifteen books of poetry, nonfiction, and fiction (short stories and novels). His work has been translated into ten languages and has received high praise from readers and literary critics for over three decades. In *The National Post,* Mark Medley calls Heighton "as good a short story writer in this country as anyone not named Munro" and "the best (living) author never to have won a Giller Prize." As a devotee of Canadian Literature and a fan who races out to buy each new Heighton book, I agree with Medley's assessment. During the January 2020 talk, I could feel the shared admiration in the room as we were treated to an intimate, energetic engagement with Heighton's rare and inspiring talent, his deeply empathetic and compassionate vision. He cast a spell over the audience; enthralled, we absorbed his exploration of the mathematical intricacies of language and the constant evolution of self. I am pleased that this new collaboration between AU's writer-in-residence program and AU Press now makes Heighton's essay available to a wider audience.

A COMMON MISCONCEPTION IS THAT an essay that is easy to read must have been easy to write. *The Virtues of Disillusionment* — with its conversational tone, compelling exploration, and intimate voice — reads so smoothly that a reader might be forgiven for almost failing to notice the rigour of intellectual exploration, the depth of knowledge, and the range of references. Heighton seems effortlessly erudite, casually drawing on insights gleaned from Zeno of Elea, Sylvia Plath, S.N. Goenka, Leonard Cohen, Laurence Durrell, Leo Tolstoy, Kate Chopin, F. Scott Fitzgerald, and Thich Nhat Hanh. Packing so much wisdom into such little space seems, to this reader and writer, magical.

However, I do not want to over-emphasize the intellectual and spiritual gravitas of this essay. Readers are about to discover that Heighton is as funny as he is smart. His clever and witty turns of phrase and his humorously original ways of seeing add to the pleasure of this reading experience. In sharing the story of his debut novel, *The Shadow Boxer,* coming out at a time of unprecedented attention for our country's literary arts, Heighton refers to himself as an entry in "the great chicken raffle of 1990s CanLit."[1] Heighton can entertain and delight even while discussing the mechanics of prefixes. "Un-," he tells us, is a "fridge magnet you clip onto the front of a word to invert its meaning."[2] As I first read the essay, I found myself smiling at one sentence, laughing aloud at another, and then, in the next moment, rethinking the very foundations of my literary career and entire life.

1   p. 9.
2   p. 5.

I copied this phrase, about our capacity for denial and avoidance, to paste above my desk: "Anything, anything not to be wakened from our obstinate trance, not to be forced to reconsider, to work hard, to start over, after demolishing the very house we live inside."[3] The phrase works as a daily reminder to be vigilant of my own houses that need demolishing. Heighton's essay makes me want not only to be a better writer and reader and thinker, but also to be a better person, to be better at living.

The Virtues of Disillusionment is a powerful and transformative essay and a perfect offering to launch this series of AU Press books derived from our writer-in-residence talks. I have read the essay many times and find new revelations to admire with each visit. I like to begin my writing day by rereading Heighton's words and carrying his insights forward into my own creative work. I trust that other readers and writers will find the essay as inspiring and uplifting as I do.

Thank you, AU Press. Thank you, Steven Heighton.

Angie Abdou
JUNE 2020

3 p. 25.

THE
VIRTUES
OF
DIS
ILLUSION
MENT

Always begin with a mystery — in this case an equation that for some reason doesn't equate, or doesn't seem to. Or call it a paradox of the kind that Zeno of Elea, the Ancient Greek philosopher and cognitive provocateur, might have appreciated.

A basic principle of both arithmetic and language is that two negatives multiplied — or, in the case of words, compounded — yield a positive. The simple math operation $(-1) \times (-1)$ gives $+1$ every time. Likewise, combine the negative prefix "un-" with a pejorative term like "burden" and the result is a semantic positive: the verb "unburden," to relieve someone or something of a physical or conceptual load. Of course, language is not math. Word meanings are contextual and often equivocal. All the same, if you tell us, "I'm not unhappy with x or y," we can be pretty sure you mean, more or less, "I'm happy with x or y," or at least "I'm content/satisfied/feel OK about x or y."

But now let's look at one of the only, and perhaps the most psychologically telling, double-negative paradoxes in English. We can set up this mystery disequation by agreeing that the word "illusion" is almost always construed as a negative term — or, in semantic terminology, a pejorative. You never tell anyone "I think you're trapped in an illusion" and mean it as a compliment. Even if your motives are benign — say, you're trying to coach or console a heartbroken friend through a divorce or other disappointment — you're still warning the person about a problem, an issue, a toxic psychic phenomenon. You're telling your friend he's clinging to a false conception; you're saying she's bought into a lie, a delusion.

We all accept or create illusions and cling to them. Anyone outside the walls of an ashram or Zen monastery — and, come to think of it, most of those inside as well — stumble hypnotized through their lives, lured and at the same time sedated by their illusions, mistaking figments and projections for reality.

In several Asian religious traditions, and in the Sanskrit language of their source scriptures, illusion is *maya*, a noun at times personified as a kind of spirit performing a many-veiled dance. She, or he, or them — the gender of the embodiment is irrelevant — is a deceiver, a decoyer, a confidence trickster, a caster of spells and weaver of

4

entrapping webs. Even teachers who embrace Buddhist principles of non-judgment warn that the illusions we cling to are limiting and damaging — hence negative. Sure, you can talk about "harmless illusions" and be understood, but the fact that the term in this usage requires a neutralizing qualifier is revealing. Illusion is, pure and simple, a minus one.

What about the other side of my paradoxical equation, the prefix "dis-"? Its Latin root means simply "not," or "un-," and in modern English the term works the same way. It's a little tag or module of negation, a valence-reverser, a semantic fridge magnet you clip onto the front of a word to invert its meaning. Mathematically speaking, it's a minus sign. *Dis*proof, *dis*order, *dis*grace; *dis*please, *dis*obey, *dis*enchant.

If we agree that "illusion" is a negative and the prefix "dis-" a kind of minus sign, then logically and by mathematical analogy "disillusion" and "disillusionment" must be positives, no? And yet in common parlance they're anything but.[1]

---

1 Kingston writer Tom Carpenter reports that many years ago, at a philosophy colloquium, a visiting scholar pointed out that while a double negative always gives a positive, a double positive will never give a negative. At which some lightning-witted wag at the back of the room heckled, "Yeah, yeah."

FOR THE SAKE OF ARGUMENT, and in accordance with logic, let's suppose now that "disillusionment" *is* in fact a positive term defining something good and desirable. What, then, could create the impression (in fact, the illusion) that it's a hateful condition you'll want to avoid at all costs?

"Warren was a weary, disillusioned man." Or, "The last time I saw her, Irina seemed depressed, regretful, disillusioned." These sentences are readily understandable, and any reader who isn't sociopathic will instantly empathize with both Warren and Irina. Everyone over a certain (very young) age has endured disillusionment and knows it to be an acutely painful sensation. "Sensation" is not nearly a strong enough word. We're talking about a pain that can suffuse our very cells and rapidly metastasize into depression; a pain that seems, symptomatically, to have much in common with the knock-out body blow that a jilting, an abandonment, or other rejection can inflict. Perhaps disillusionment is a *kind* of jilting/rejection? It can leave us feeling we've been dropped by the world, existentially dumped; the cherished belief we were embracing like a lover has turned out to be a cheat, a false friend, a zero, and the pain of that epiphany is lonely and isolating.

To be disillusioned is to be Dear Johned by a spectre. There we stand, ears scalding with shame as we realize how grotesquely we'd given ourselves to the illusion that something about ourselves or the world was true.[2]

---

2 Some latter-day Linnaeus needs to spreadsheet a comprehensive Taxonomy of Sorrow. There are so many kinds. And yet it might be the case that most are closely related — most arising from a sense of exclusion and relegation in various forms. Rejection by a lover, your community, your employer, maybe the publisher you send a book to after three years of work, maybe the public that seems to reject that book if it actually is published. Of course, the level of pain sustained can differ greatly, from dismay to full depression, depending on your life context, your degree of equanimity, your support network, and the severity of the rejection itself. But the chemical markers in the mind and body are the same, and the corresponding feelings as we describe them to each other seem similar. Which should be no surprise; it stands to reason that social animals would evolve to feel and fear, hence try to avoid, exclusion, exposure, banishment, etc.

The pain of bereavement might be an outlier. While the various sorrows of spurning seem to diminish and demote us — make us feel like solitary "losers" — bereavement/grief can induce a very different feeling. An often-rejected person might, after a bereavement, feel *less* excluded than usual, hence less lonely, because — if all goes well — friends, family and community come together at the funeral to grieve. Yes, that's part of it; while the other sorrows stem from a sense of exclusion or abandonment, grief can and should be a shared, communal emotion ... The other difference is that a stillbirth, say, or the death of an 88-year-old parent, doesn't make you feel like a failure but simply like someone who has suffered a loss. And while there's such a thing as survivor guilt, there's also survivor gratitude. You walk away from the graveside bereft but alive.

I FIRST NOTICED the mathematical/logical singularity of "disillusionment" some years ago, but I didn't understand the implications then. It simply struck me as a pleasing paradox, an interesting little insight, and I must have thought I was clever to note it. But I did nothing *about* it. It didn't change the way I lived or the way I regarded — failed to recognize, I should say — my own illusions.

It was in 1996, in the weeks before my first child, a daughter, was born. I was trying to finish the first draft of a first novel. I was writing fast, by hand, around 2,500 rough words a day, inspired by a sense of both urgency and excitement. Urgency because I wanted to get the first draft down before the child came and upended my life, as everyone warned me would happen; excitement because this novel-in-progress was to be the first book in a so-called "two-book deal" I'd recently signed with my first big publisher.

My publisher seemed excited too. The mid-90s was a time when the larger presses in Canada began dispensing relatively generous advances to young, sometimes all but unpublished, writers, partly out of real literary enthusiasm but also in hopes of getting lucky with a lucrative young star. My new publisher — effectively pestered by one of the savvy international agents now arriving on the scene, and persuaded by the reviews I'd gotten for my first couple of books — ponied up and purchased me as one of their tickets in the great chicken raffle of 1990s CanLit. My agent, my publisher, my friends, my colleagues (especially, I see now, the colleagues who disliked me) all assured me I was on the brink of a brilliant success. That sounded nice. Above all, though, I was delighted about the cash advance that helped buy me at least another year of full-time writing and stabilized my income at exactly the moment I was starting a family.

ILLUSIONS ARE A BAD THING, we can agree, but can they sometimes be useful? In *The Alexandria Quartet* Lawrence Durrell, sampling a key tenet of Buddhist scripture, writes, "Personality as something with fixed attributes is an illusion — but a necessary illusion if we are to love!" And maybe illusions in the form of mental formations and obsessions are necessary to creative artists, at least at a certain stage of their development. Some years ago, the Canadian literary journal *The New Quarterly* asked writers for a piece of advice they wished someone had murmured in the ear of their younger selves. Realizing how woefully ignorant I'd been when starting out, I came up with *seventeen* pieces of advice to be stuffed into a reverse time capsule and wormholed back to me. Those seventeen "memos" then turned into a whole book. The first memo reads, "Interest is never enough. If it doesn't haunt you, you'll never write it well. What haunts and obsesses you into writing may, with luck and labour, interest your readers. What merely interests you is sure to bore them."[3]

This memo offers a pseudo-mathematical equation of its own. It argues that mere interest — after suffering the subtraction of energy that occurs in the inexact translation of emotions into abstract signifiers on a page — ends up a mere cipher. Only obsession, with its unique degree of psychic power, can survive that process of subtraction and remain a significant sum on the page, and in your reader's imagination. This memo, then, implies a wish: if only as a younger writer I'd been better at distinguishing between mere curiosity and haunting obsession. If only I'd been better able to locate my true material.

Luckily it does get easier with time and practice — i.e., time and repeated failure. And though obsession is not synonymous with illusion, there's a good deal of overlap.

3 Heighton, *Workbook: Memos & Dispatches on Writing* (Toronto: ECW, 2011), p. 21.

So writing well — writing into, and out of, your obsessions — means engaging with your cherished illusions and, who knows, maybe one day fully exorcizing them.[4]

INNER DEMONS can drive creative work, no question, but the issue for any creative artist (especially, I suspect, those of a Romantic bent) is to decide how long you want to host and harness the ghosts that drive you and feed your art.[5] At what point is the daily price of possession too high to pay? Should you go into therapy, onto medication, to a Vipassanā mindfulness retreat? Will a bipolar artist's work suffer if she starts taking a drug that snips off the extremes of her moods at both poles? Or will such a protocol simply help her survive so as to continue making her art, even at a slightly less febrile pitch? What would

4   As a courtesy to readers who, like me, resent trying to follow arguments bereft of examples ... A creatively productive obsession might be a fear of abandonment stemming from — surprise, surprise — some childhood trauma; a closely related illusion might be a sense of unworthiness, the illogical belief that one deserves and is destined to be abandoned. The obsession is the *fear;* the illusion is the *belief,* the explanatory and rationalizing apparatus that, unfortunately, locks the obsession into place, often for a lifetime.

5   Or how long you want to focus on *them* instead of the less dramatic, less pathological sources of inspiration a Romantic might find it easy to overlook or ignore.

Sylvia Plath's *Ariel* poems be without the obsessive grief, fury, despair, the insomnia and barbiturates?

Such difficult questions are beyond the scope of any one essay. Let's stay concrete and look at a simple example that requires no set-up. In *Moby-Dick*, Herman Melville's protagonist, Captain Ahab, fanatically pursues a sperm whale that to him seems to constitute some deeply disturbing affront, perhaps the horror of a world created and then abandoned by an absentee god. Melville observes and describes that obsessive quest with some degree of authorial objectivity and control — and yet if he weren't at least a little *possessed* by the whale and the pursuit, why would he and how could he have kept it all going for over 200,000 words?[6] Likewise by the end of *The Great Gatsby* — another familiar, obvious example — the reader can't help but feel that the author, F. Scott Fitzgerald, is or has been as obsessed as Gatsby with "the green light, the orgiastic future" — in short, the American Dream of happiness-pursued that draws Gatsby on to his doom.

If these writers hadn't fundamentally understood, and partly shared and wrestled with, the illusions of their protagonists, the novels might have been mere entertainments or, on the other hand, academic exercises — schematic exposés of pathological mind-states.

---

6 No fewer than 1,685 of which are "whale."

Art instead demands the submersion of the artist in the material; anyone exposing an illusion must be at least partly enthralled by it.

Maybe every artist starts out possessed and then, in the process of creating, partly transcends the obsession, exorcises the demon or ghost.

WHICH BRINGS US TO Leonard Cohen. I believe much of his best work was fuelled by the pursuit of two illusions: fame and a kind of transfiguring erotic atonement. In a 1993 television interview with Barbara Gowdy he suggested that "more or less over the years" he had been down on his knees before women. In other words, praying and worshipping while making love. Nothing wrong with that; surely that's how eros at its most nourishing should be. And Cohen is hardly alone. Since the advent of courtly love and its direct descendant, Romanticism, countless poets and singers have displaced religious feelings onto sexual love (along with art). But some ultimate, transcendent consummation, an erotic apotheosis, is not a human possibility; the hallelujah of each orgasm is by nature fleeting, even if its afterglow of felt connection to another being can be sustaining and anchoring.

Still, as Ahab seeks Ultimate Reality by pursuing Leviathan, Cohen (or at least his persona: the spiritual equivalent of a *nom de plume*) seeks it through the bodies of lovers. In one of his last songs, Cohen declares that for years he was fighting with temptation but didn't want to win. "A man like me," he sings, "doesn't like to see temptation caving in." And yet, he finds, it has. Here an artist who has been gripped and inspired by a powerful illusion *acknowledges* the illusion, the pain of losing his muse and his fuel.

And yet Cohen's last album before his death, *You Want It Darker,* is one of his best and was rightly acclaimed as such. The passing of an illusion, it seems, can generate art as good as the illusion itself.

IN THE ECHOING, skylit central atrium of the Museum of Illusions, two unimpressive, in fact pathetic, specimens lie on eternal display. The immense hall is otherwise empty. Brass plaques, apparently of some antiquity, identify the two as embalmed avatars of the two primary human illusions, one internal, one external.

Exhibit A is little more than layers of stained mummy wraps collapsing over the feeble armature of a few cracked ribs. The skull — more simian than human — is a husk. Blindly staring eyeholes.

This silent shell is what remains of a thing that was once pharaonically, anabolically self-important (though at times abject, self-pitying), often loud, anxious for attention, hyperactively craving or fearing, loving or hating, judging, opining, squinting ahead or glancing back in time hopefully, apprehensively, regretfully — a manic, moody little chatterbox. It believed religiously, jealously in its own separate, solid existence. It insisted the world believe too!

What went wrong here?

The hermetic case can't fully contain a sharp whiff of failure.

Ego's assignment was straightforward. It was to act as an interface, to negotiate with the world on behalf of the person, the mind, the Self. But Ego's filibustering chatter, external and internal, came to drown out the intimations of the Self and the murmurs of the nightmind. Egged on and abetted by a culture of egoistic individualism, Ego came to believe it was more than just a key facet of the Self — the mind's agent, advocate, reasoner, day-manager, tactician, translator — it *was* the Self. Not just a conductor and stage crew but also composer and orchestra.

Like the AI that seizes power in dystopian fiction, Ego staged a coup.

But like anyone who has seized power, Ego existed in a state of constant vigilance and insecurity. How it hated losing control in the small hours, when it could no longer silence the subversive nightmind: that Dadaist working by candlelight while the brownshirts sleep in their barracks.

How obsessively Ego feared death, that ultimate counter-coup and loss of control — a democratic affront to its being. So it set about self-bunkering, self-fortressing, always reviewing the past and scanning the future, fretting and hoping, patrolling the perimeter ...

It's Ego, ever-uncertain, that makes you stick with what you know and repeat the same social and psychic strategies, useful or not. It's Ego that compels you to seek approval, so you find yourself going along with other egos (all likewise seeking a putative security-through-approval) when they push you toward a goal you sense you don't want, to marry someone you fear you don't love, to deny your true sexual nature, to participate in a shunning ... Meanwhile that deeper you, a hostage in its own house, is trying to warn you awake, to bypass the dictator's guards with notes in the coded form of inklings, spasms of conscience, or, if all else fails, disturbing dreams, those insistent screams of the subconscious.[7] A usurper never free of the anxiety of its imposture, Ego remains reactive, testy, never far from its next tantrum, its throne a large high chair. It shakes a fist at the sky,

---

7 Another paradox. The self-isolating Ego is generally far less independent and more anxiously conformist than the deep Self with its anarchic tendencies ... The Self seeks a larger destiny, and not for the sake of success-by-worldly-metrics but for the sake of psychic fulfillment, which is a form of truth, of potential realized over time.

indignant that non-existent gods fail to fulfill its every demand. The jesters must juggle for it *now*. The generals must announce fresh conquests. The court players will perform the same slightly revised scenes with the same gratifying endings ... While the Self finds wonder even in loss and decay, and takes joy in planting trees whose shade it will never sit beneath, Ego stays clenched against the miracle. Ego wants its fruit now — and wants credit for planting the tree. While the nightmind scribbles odes to the earth and its cycles, Ego snaps a selfie and asks, Does this make me look old?

THE NEIGHBOURING GLASS CASE contains an even sorrier relic. Surely, you think, the curators could be trying harder? Here lies the Pursuit of Happiness — the primary external illusion — beloved, coddled love-child of the first, so carefully nurtured, protected at all costs, so deeply and lastingly...

Except there was no child. No birth. Only a false pregnancy, one of those cases where a desperately hopeful mother believes she has conceived, presents with all the outward symptoms, but then in the end her belly, distended with air, deflates like a bubble.

So this elaborate coffer with its plaque, spotlighting, and internal ventilation system is in fact empty. Of course. If the mummy in case number one was a false self —

a figment — what else could we expect to find? Exhibit B is a dream hatched in the mind of a dream.

As if a ghost had straddled a grave to give birth.

This is what's left of the great Ponzi scheme of pursuable happiness.

It's possible to feel happy, of course, even to describe oneself as a happy person. The illusion lies in believing that the word "happiness" signifies something concrete, like "loam" or "granite," not abstract and ambiguous like "glory" or "truth" or "hope." As if it denotes a solid, stable, *terminal* reality, a place where you can arrive and stay, or something you can catch and keep in the form of the right spouse, body weight, income, number of online followers … And note how Ego, in hunting happiness, obsesses over metrics, comparative numbers, a math crudely limited to grade school functions like addition, subtraction, division, multiplication: (Daisy Buchanan) + (lots of money) + (West Egg) = (Success-and-respect) = (Happiness). And if the illusions continue to recede and elude us, as Gatsby's creator writes in his famous closing, "No matter, tomorrow we will run faster, go farther …"

But just who, or what, is it that's scurrying in pursuit here, slipping off the back of the treadmill? Just as the dream of terminal happiness turned out to be a phantom's fantasy, here too a ghost is on the heels of a ghost. "Ego" believes that reaching and embracing "happiness" will somehow solidify it, reify it, make it permanent and undying. But 0 + 0 will always still = 0.

<hr/>

TO BE SPECIFIC AGAIN. The dream of happiness-through-fame, i.e., limitless attention — clearly that too is a game of ghost-tag, inasmuch as fame, like money, doesn't guarantee the contentment we naturally associate with both. (The cruel paradox here: while neither success nor wealth can ensure happiness, failure and poverty are likely to induce the opposite.)

But for an artist there is one very useful thing about the Great White Whale or Holy Grail of fame: it keeps you in the studio recording, or in your workshed painting, or at your desk writing. Your ultimate goal might be to reach a state of maturity and enlightenment where the satisfaction of work done well is enough to keep you creating, but in the decades before you reach that point, a simple desire for attention and respect, to say nothing of money earned, can be a helpful inducement.[8]

---

8 The current American president is a good example of a person whose pursuit is not so much of money and power, which he was born with and hence takes for granted, but *attention* — a commodity without which his kind feel themselves stripped and spectralized. The privacy and anonymity that many rich folks crave would entail, for him, erasure: a subtraction to zero.

THE PROTAGONIST OF my first novel, *The Shadow Boxer*, is a young guy who grows up in a northern town and ends up going down to the big city — Toronto, in his case — to try to "make it" as a writer. Like the hero of any Bildungsroman, he is seeking both Success and Love as conventionally defined.

At the time I wrote the first draft I was about ten years older than the protagonist and, as I mentioned, about to become a father. In other words, I was a decade farther down the road. But I couldn't have written about my hero's "quest" with any authenticity if I hadn't shared his obsessions when I'd been his age — and if I *still* wasn't driven by them while writing.

Yet as I look back now, I can see I already understood that he and I were gripped by illusions that were unhealthy. This must be why I wrote, in the first draft's concluding pages,

How was it that both "illusion" and its opposite, "disillusion," could mean negative things? To drop illusions should be a good thing, yet when push came to shove you never gave them up happily. Each one had to be frayed, through struggle and blunder, to a painful thinness, then stripped away with violence, a scale of still-living cells.

In a sense I was trying to give my protagonist — in some ways my even younger self — a memo of advice. Yet I wasn't applying the advice in my own life. Clearly, I still believed or hoped that success could transform me — that it was not in fact an ungraspable, shifting, fickle thing but instead a concrete destination I could reach and then reside in securely. In other words, I was fighting with temptation, but I didn't want to win.

Then again, who ever takes their own good advice?

Still, it seems strange that you can know something to be true and then, for decades, not fully *live* it. In fact, trying to find that short passage I just quoted, I had to skim a number of pages in my old reading copy of *The Shadow Boxer* and was repeatedly surprised by the book's insights. Did I really know that much about life back then? I barely know it now. And if I did know those things then, why couldn't I apply them? And how can I possibly *still* not be applying some of them two decades later?

Dig out an old diary from high school or even grade school and you'll be even more shocked by the occasional glints of genuine insight flashing up from among all the dross and detritus. Maybe early in life we do know, or at least suspect, most of what we need to know, then simply forget or fail to enact it.

The Shadow Boxer was to be published in the spring of 2000. My publisher honoured its promises and got behind the book, obviously keen to push it and make it a hit. They were prepping ads for the big newspapers — a marketing measure that even twenty years ago was not all that common — while sending out scores of review copies and setting up interviews with newspapers and magazines. They had garnered some flattering blurbs from big names in CanLit. The advance buzz — i.e., ignorant consensus of folks who mostly hadn't read the thing — was encouraging. As a writer friend said at the time, "I think you're on the cusp."

The cusp of what? I should have asked.

BY THE END OF *The Shadow Boxer* my protagonist's own first novel — a novel within a novel called "The Islands of the Nile" — has fallen apart and failed, like his other lazy, romantic dreams. His life, at least the false life he has been constructing, collapses. He files for a kind of emotional bankruptcy.

And *does* he go on to take his creator's advice about the virtues of disillusionment? Hard to say, but at last sight we see him living less manically — more intentionally — and assuming responsibility for a child he has fathered. He's slowly, more attentively rereading all the Western classics he'd mainlined as a teenager, when he was absorbing their style but not grasping their lessons. Disabused of his less useful illusions, he seems a grown-up at last.

Failure, it seems, has been the making of him.

But while I wanted my character to grow up through disillusionment, apparently I didn't really want that for myself. In early May 2000, while in Toronto for interviews, I was chuffed when a media friend confided that my first big review, due in a few days, was a rave that urged everyone to go out and buy or shoplift the book.

DISABUSED OF HIS *less useful illusions.* I find that word, "disabuse," a powerful and intriguing one. The *Concise* OED gives two definitions: to free from a mistaken idea, or to disillusion. So the word is a straight-up synonym for "disillusion" while having the advantage of not confusing the issue, semantically and psychologically, via a double negative that still somehow yields a negative. Because both *dis-* and *abuse* — clearly minus ones — do, when fused together, correctly yield a positive. Or so I'd argue. True, being disabused of an illusion might be a painful process, but the word itself implies a kind of liberation from some form of abuse. And if cherished illusions are in a sense self-administered, the word implies further that our attachment to them is a form of *self*-abuse.

Which raises yet another implication. Could clinging to illusions be a form of substance abuse — our illusion-attachments a kind of addiction?

The more I ponder the possibility, the clearer it seems that illusion-attachments simply *are* addictions, and possibly even more tenacious than addictions to external substances like alcohol, nicotine, methamphetamine, or opioids. After all, the roots of the abuse run far deeper — often back to early childhood — and so the correlative neural circuitry is fundamentally grooved, our addiction to the associated bodily chemicals deeply entrenched.

As with opioids, the drug's ultimate purpose was to sedate the mind and ease pain.

Disillusionment is a state of withdrawal from a long-abused substance. No wonder it hurts like hell. No wonder it can scar or kill you.[9]

THE FIRST BIG REVIEW of *The Shadow Boxer* was indeed a rave, but others were mixed and rightfully so. The novel was flawed in the ways that most first novels are flawed. I'd believed that nailing every word to the page and sustaining intense verbal energy over 400 pages would suffice

---

9 Our society is sick in a double sense. Most of us are either addicted to dangerous illusions or in a state of painful withdrawal from them. In other words, we're illusioned and disillusioned at the same time. And we keep getting tempted into seeking relief from dubious sources: most recently and obviously, through social media and its lottery-promise of viral fame.

to make for an excellent novel. But those factors guaranteed only that the book was vivid and alive.

Some of the mixed reviews diagnosed structural and tonal flaws (in the book's middle section) that I had sensed while writing the book — issues that a few pre-readers had also tactfully flagged but that I, attached to my romantic illusion that dynamic style conquered all and my natural hope that the book would be both great and a hit, had denied, downplayed, or talked myself out of. As we tend to do when our dearest illusions are challenged. Anything, anything not to be wakened from our obstinate trance, not to be forced to reconsider, to work harder, to start over, after demolishing the very house we live inside.

The pain of waking to self-awareness might be likened to that of coming to with the most crushing hangover of your life, but I suspect a better analogy is the shock and trauma of being born.

THE BOOK ACTUALLY SOLD DECENTLY, but not enough to earn back my advance. It created a certain post-publication "buzz" but didn't win any of the big prizes that are now, and were even then, essential to a perception of success. By the end of 2000 the media consensus seemed to be that the book was notable but not the big thing that many had predicted and for which others had hoped.

"HOPE" is the next word I want to consider mathematically. We'd probably all agree, initially, that it's a term with a positive value. Renowned Buddhist philosopher Thich Nhat Hanh, however, begs to differ. On the contrary, he says he perceives something tragic in hope.

Most readers, on first encountering that notion, will feel surprised and incredulous, even indignant. I know I did. The statement is counterintuitive, paradoxical — a quiet provocation that inverts a word's valence from positive to negative. How can *hope* be negative?

Hopefulness, Nhat Hanh suggests, is a harmful emotion because it's based on an illusion. A hope is not something real that exists but rather a wish that something might exist — or might disappear if it now exists. Unlike the present moment, which is real and occurring, hope is speculative, an abstraction projected into the future. And by hoping ourselves into the future, we miss out on the good things — miracles, few though they might be — happening even now, despite our problems.

The basis of hope is biological. Any creature registering a lack, or pain, is being alerted about a deviation from homeostasis that it needs to correct — a response vector without which it would not survive long. But while non-human creatures act to end negative stimuli as soon as possible, the human mind's roster of responses is various and, at times, maladaptive. To hope for change or relief instead of acting now is sometimes necessary (e.g., so as not to get fired or jailed) but often damaging. What's more, early in life we learn to equate any form of unease —some of it potentially instructive, most of it fleeting — with pain-as-urgent-physical-warning or as potentially-permanent-condition, so we grow into a state of comprehensive, at times constant, aversion and hope for relief.

Which is to crave the impossible: a struggle-free life in a world governed by the second law of thermodynamics, a world where all things are subject to entropy. Our flu, back spasms, or spiking anxiety might subside, but something will come along to replace them. In the meantime, conjecturing ourselves past our distress robs us of the one thing we truly have: this moment and the potential for action and change that exists here and here alone.

As every athlete finds out, action contaminated by hope (*if only I can nail this next serve ... I'll win if I nail this next serve!*) usually fails. Hope is a fatal distraction. It creates a kind of skip, jitter, or satellite delay in the nerves. Where there's hope, there's fear, their relationship an alternating current. On the other hand, a play or movement executed in a fully present, fearless frame of mind — without hope — often succeeds.[10]

10 That is, in a state that's *hope-free* as opposed to *hopeless*.

Worst of all, hopefulness — that "if only!" state of mind — becomes a mental habit that does not just go away once things improve a little or a lot. The relief of every hope realized creates a new hope/fear. So we go on, slinging ourselves ahead of ourselves toward death, in fact hastening its approach, our actual lives left uninhabited.

What is hope, in the end, but the antipodal twin of memory? A bright mirage projected on the clouds ahead, like a distorted image of the mirages cast on the clouds behind? We spend our lives framed, hemmed in by these dense fog banks, rarely realizing we're alive in the sunlit space between. Or: we're like drivers at night, barely registering a never-heard-before song on the speakers or cherishing the sleep-breathing of the passenger beside us as we squint ahead to where our high beams diffuse into fog, fearing a collision or watching for a sign, then checking the rearview yet again, ruminating on the rose-lit or blood-lit dimness behind. A prudent protocol for driving, maybe, but no way to live.

FOR A FEW YEARS I've been pondering a marvellous German compound noun — *Lebenslüge*, or life-lie, the convenient if sometimes fatal fiction around which you build your life. And here, too, I see what could be construed as a signif-icant verbal equation.

The compound is built out of *Leben*, life, and *Lüge*, lie. A *Lebenslüge*, in my own elaboration of the term, is a primary illusion around which other, lesser illusions constellate. Naturally the term can also be applied in a larger, collective way, suggesting the lie or illusion around which a nation shapes its identity. The American life-lie is the belief in American exceptionalism: Land of the Free, the Greatest Nation on Earth, etc. The Canadian life-lie is the fantasy that we're the good ones, the nice guys, fundamentally better than Americans or Brits because, allegedly, we're innocent of such atrocities as slavery, empire-building, and Indigenous genocide.

The life-lie of Canadian niceness has, it's safe to say, been outed as an illusion, yet even now, in the wake of the Residential Schools exposé, it seems many of us continue to believe that We the North are somehow "nicer." We resist disillusionment so as to save face, to save the appearances, to shore up the foundations of a house of smoke and shadows. The truth hurts, as false friends — or "frenemies" — sometimes say when they turn on us and tactlessly point out our flaws. But what hurts worse than a painful truth is a lie outed, especially one we've been telling ourselves.

Worse is discovering we're our own frenemies.

Worst of all is discerning, over the course of many sleepless nights, that you have not one life-lie but many —

a webwork of illusions that over the years you've told yourself about yourself (whatever "I" and "myself" might be, or whatever they once were, if they ever were at all).

<hr>

THE PROTAGONISTS OF all good novels must discover their *Lebenslügen*, or at least approach closely before recoiling, disillusioned, having granted the reader a glimpse. I think this is pretty much a hard and fast rule of literature. Likewise writers — the creators of those protagonists — can hope to get closer to their own life-lies over the course of a book's composition and through the agency of those characters. Yet it might take a writer a trilogy of novels, or a lifetime's work, to fully arrive there. Protagonists, after all, can be forced to realize what their creators still cleverly manage not to acknowledge and face.

But the obsessions/illusions that fuel a young writer's work can, in an older writer, become mere blockages manifesting on the page as repetitive, self-plagiarizing tropes and patterns. A writer's work must be the treatment by which her obsessions are gradually unpacked, metabolized, transcended.

One problem with early success is that it can cajole an artist — naturally eager for a follow-up fix of addictive celebrity — to stagnate in an inchoate stage.

To be sure, the liberation of disillusionment comes too late for some protagonists. As Leo Tolstoy's profoundly disabused heroine walks toward the fatal train station in the last section of *Anna Karenina*, she hears the Vespers bells ringing and asks rhetorically why they ring. "To disguise the fact that we all hate one another," she concludes. In other words, the bells ring for the same reason we chatter emptily to someone we don't much like at a party. To drown out the sound of our true feelings; to avoid being disliked; to avoid being snubbed or shunned.

Note too that this moment, which contains arguably the most important insight in the novel, is never mentioned, never quoted — not by Tolstoy scholars, not by the reviewers of new translations, not by lay readers. It's the forgotten truth of one of the world's most closely read texts. But after all, who *wants* to know that we human primates, in our less wakened state, are driven more by envy, spite, and hatred than by love? In fact, until our cloud-chateaux implode and we start to rebuild on solid ground, we don't know what real love is.

As philosopher and canidophile Mark Rowlands puts it, "An ape is always on the make."

LATE IN 2019 I finished a new book and on its final page I found myself returning to the paradox of disillusionment that I first broached in *The Shadow Boxer* — though I'd long since forgotten that I'd broached it. As I wrote this new version of the idea, half-feeling I was taking dictation from some other part of my mind, it dawned on me that I'd arrived at this same place a long time ago.

This new book, a kind of memoir, was started and finished about twenty years after *The Shadow Boxer* and — more importantly — after raising a child to adulthood and losing a mother, a stillborn son, and several friends. Meanwhile I also experienced some typical midlife setbacks, failures, and disappointments, starting with the disappointment of that first novel failing to become a blockbuster.

Let me repeat that I consider myself lucky that the book did not take off; let me repeat that it didn't deserve to. I'm lucky because in the long run few things damage a career like an undeserved early hit.[11] And if premature success — as argued above — can stunt an artist's psyche, it can inflict aesthetic damage too. If a flawed product had brought me the success I'd craved, how would I have gone on to get better? Why would I have even tried?

11 Unfortunately, a well-deserved early hit can have the same effect.

Where's the incentive to push farther, to work and suffer, when sometimes-good is good enough? And getting better does require some suffering, and there are no analgesics, no shortcuts. Why transcend the grotesque delusion that you've already arrived at craft-mastery when the world is flattering you that you have, in fact, arrived? The truth is, there's no arrival, only a frighteningly, beautifully open road, the sun crowning dawn after dawn, the radio playing — and occasional rest-stops in roadside Edens.

<hr />

IN THE LAST paragraph of this new book, *Reaching Mithymna,* I put it this way:

> Everyone gets away with certain things for a while
> but no one gets away with everything forever [...]
> But if our illusions — the cherished ones above all —
> are harmful, isn't disillusionment a good thing, a
> necessary correction so painful that our word for it
> is negative? Nobody ever changes until they have to.

So here I am, twenty years later, still giving myself advice — the *same* advice — still coaching myself onward up that infinite, indefinite road. But while the concept here is similar to the one in *The Shadow Boxer,* one key point is different: that people don't change until they must, until they've suffered enough that they can't go on with the charade, the façade, the life-lie. The matchbox tower has to topple. The dancer's gauzy veils have to be torn away to reveal ... no dancer beneath, no form at all, nothing. There never was one. Not even a ghost.

In fact, there never was even a *me* or *you* that suffered all that pain. The pain itself was real, even lethal — but the solid, unchanging self that seemed to feel it was an illusion. What's more, the lie of that solid ego gave the pain a place to roost, a place to stick and fester and worsen ... And maybe this is another reason radical disillusionment hurts so terribly: it means acknowledging your own death, or the death of that thing that for years you believed was you, the false self that your life-lies were protecting.

MEMO TO SELF: the best justification for emotional pain is that the path to mature consciousness runs through a gauntlet of sorrow and loss.

All song begins with the blues.

Here too lies one of the best justifications for reading fiction: the reader is allowed, in fact forced, to witness the progressive disillusionment of a protagonist. If a novel or story casts a powerful enough spell, readers are drawn into the experience and half-live it themselves, as with Kate Chopin's *The Awakening* or John Williams's *Stoner* ... Whenever I finish such books I have a choice, as in the wake of some emotional crisis that briefly lasers the cataracts of habit and hopefulness. With my sympathies still fully provoked and churning, I can turn to face my own illusions. Or I can stall, distract myself and duly return, a re-amnesiac, to my coma of complacency.

DEVOURING NOVELS when you're young — as does the protagonist of *The Shadow Boxer* — gives you a glimpse of the necessity of liberation, but unless you're very lucky you don't instantly waken. Likewise, reading Buddhist scriptures for twenty years might make you kinder and more thoughtful, but the only thing that will foment fundamental change is subjecting the insights to disciplined practice. Knowing what's wrong — even knowing the solution — is not enough. Besides, at twenty or thirty or forty, or, in fact, fifty, sixty, older, many cling to the hope that somehow things will still work out, that eventual success, praise, sex, friends, likes and loves *will* confer a final happiness. In fact, you have to suffer enough first that you finally give up that hope. The guru S.N. Goenka grew up in a rich family in Burma and said the main reason he was grateful for it was — herewith another double negative — he never had to doubt that wealth could not buy happiness. Had he been poor, he would always have wondered if in fact those outward things *could* have saved him the work of awakening.

CONCLUDING A BOOK with an insight you wrote down two decades before … surely this represents at worst a sign of stagnation or, at best, a coming-full-circle, a closing of the door on a stage of life … or even a vindicating rematch with Maya, avatar of illusion? Maybe it's more that we need to keep rediscovering and rethinking paradoxical insights, so that decade by decade, by slow degrees, we absorb them and finally begin to act. Instant Enlightenment, after all, is another fantasy born of laziness and hope. And we're all re-amnesiacs, forever forgetting ourselves and dozing back into old habits — though perhaps a little less each time.

But a correct equation remains correct whether we forget or recall it, embrace or deny it. The double negative (dis) + (illusion) gives a positive term and the result — basic math, yet the equation can take a lifetime to learn — is freedom.

⚘ AU PRESS

Copyright © 2020 Steven Heighton
Published by AU Press, Athabasca University
1200, 10011 – 109 Street Edmonton, Alberta T5J 3S8
https://doi.org/10.15215/aupress/9781771993265.01

Book design by Natalie Olsen
Cover image © Antonova Katya
Author photo © Mark Raynes Roberts
Printed and bound in Canada

Library and Archives Canada Cataloguing in Publication
Title: The virtues of disillusionment / Steven Heighton.
Names: Heighton, Steven, author.
Identifiers: Canadiana (print) 20200284894 | Canadiana (ebook)
20200284967 | ISBN 9781771993265 (softcover) | ISBN 9781771993258 (PDF)
| ISBN 9781771993241 (EPUB) | ISBN 9781771993234 (Kindle)
Subjects: LCSH: Illusion (Philosophy) | LCSH: Negativity (Philosophy) |
LCSH: Perception. | LCSH: Satisfaction.
Classification: LCC B105.I44 H45 2020 | DDC 128—DC23

We acknowledge the financial support of the Government of Canada
through the Canada Book Fund (CBF) for our publishing activities and
the assistance provided by the Government of Alberta through the Alberta
Media Fund.

Canada Alberta
          Government

The author wishes to thank Ginger Pharand, Alexander Scala, Angie Abdou,
Tom Carpenter, Alison Gzowski, Karyn Wisselink, Pamela Holway, Megan
Hall, Natalie Olsen, Peter Midgley, and Kathy Killoh.